COLORING · NOTEBOOK

STAY WOKE

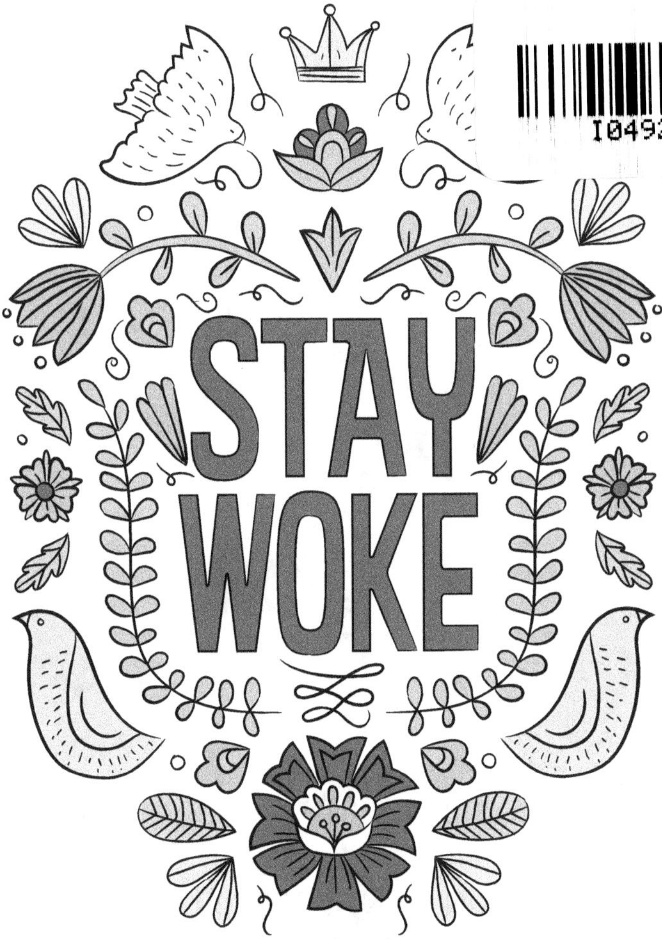

Follow on instagram @ marieriverscoloring
on facebook @ marieriverscoloring

More from Marie Rivers

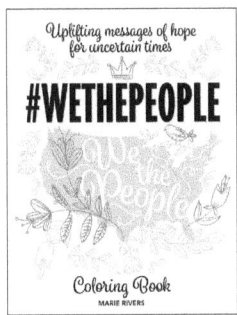

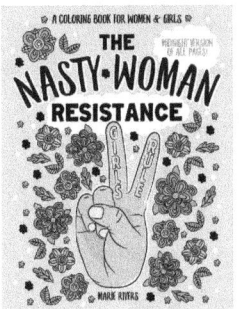

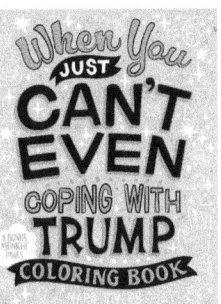

ISBN-13: 978-1724403377
ISBN-10: 1724403370

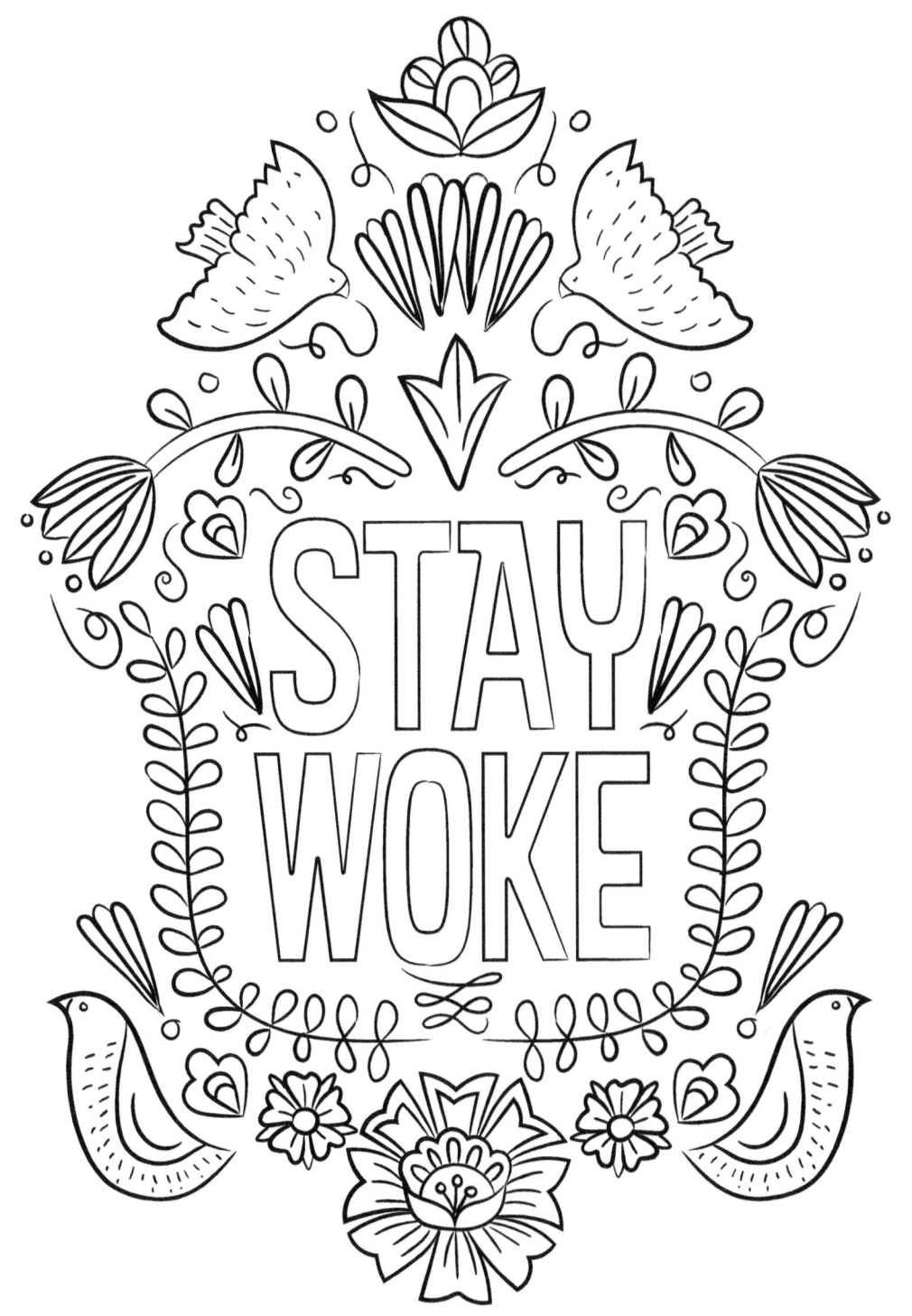

DATE: / /

DATE: / /

DATE: / /

DATE: / /

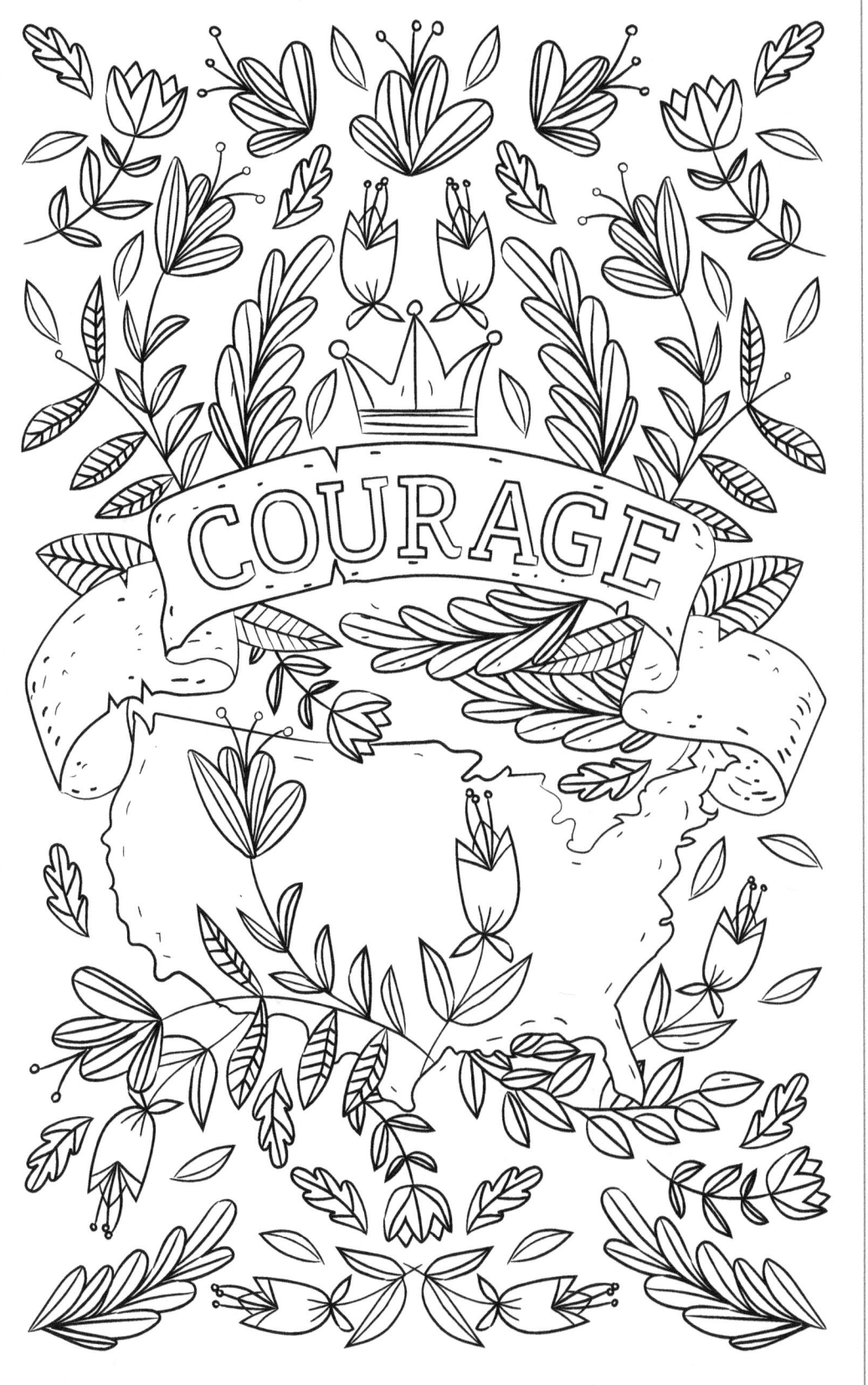

DATE: / /

DATE: /   /

DATE: / /

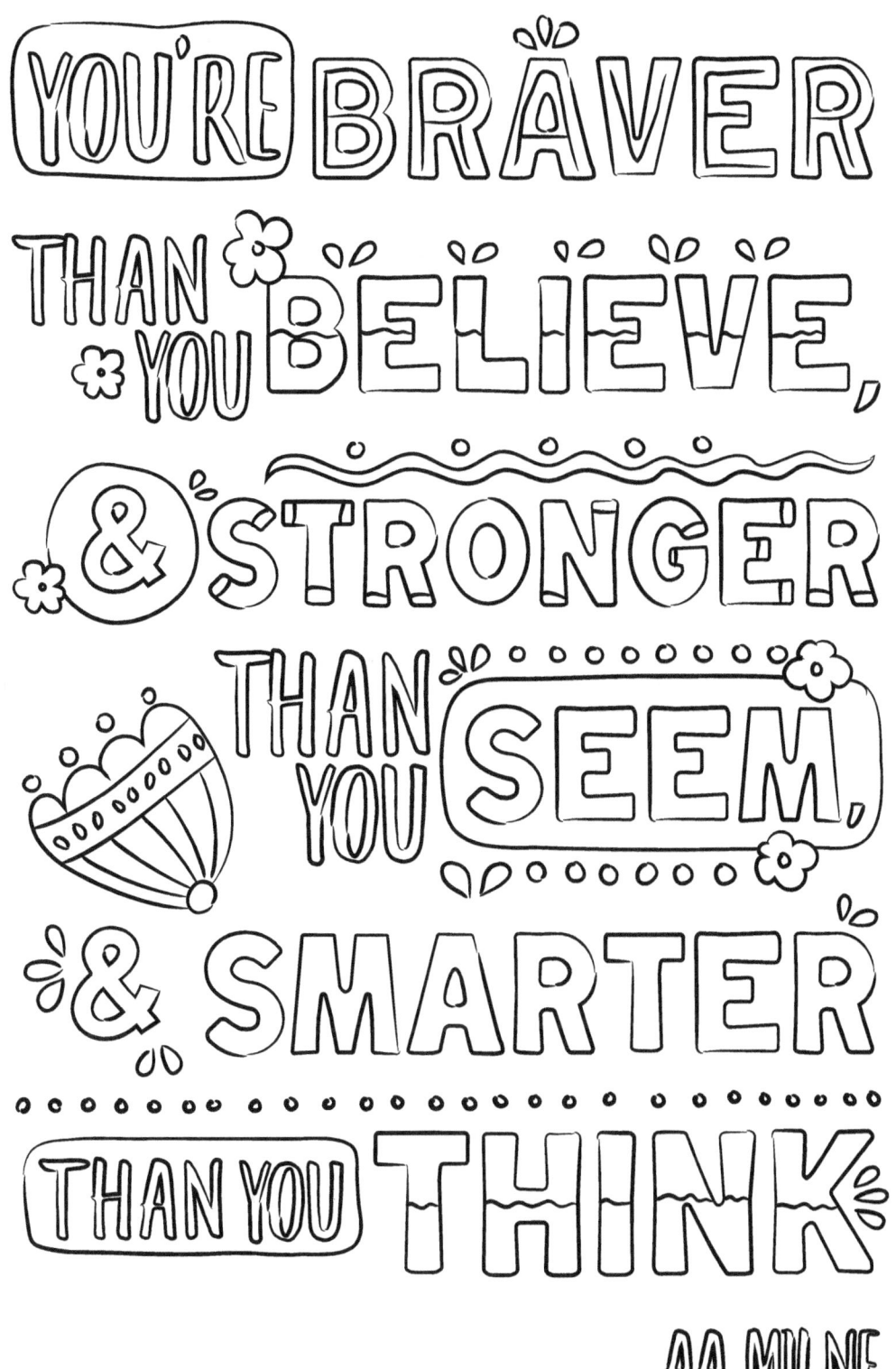

DATE: / /

I SEE THE
DARKNESS
I CHOOSE
to be the
Light

DATE: / /

DATE: ___ / ___ / ___

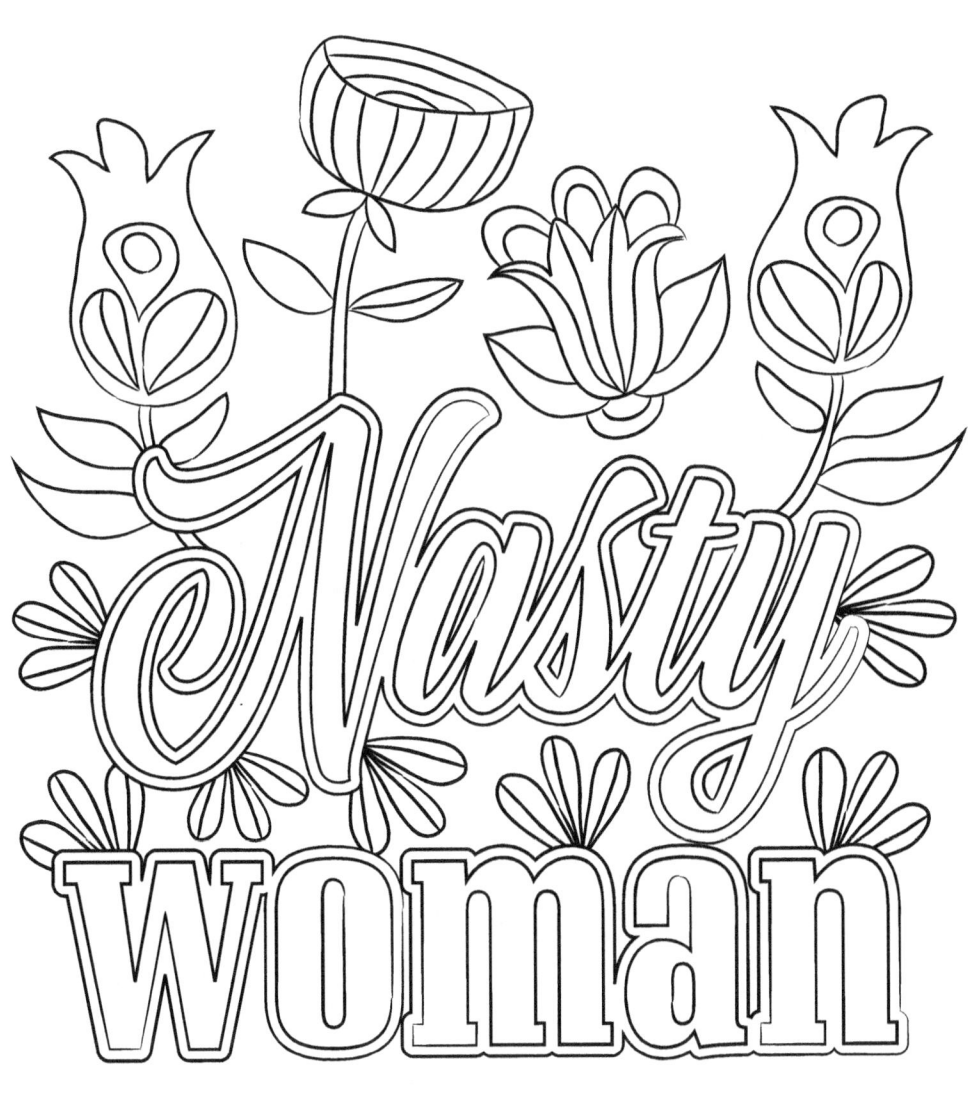

DATE: / /

DATE: / /

DATE: / /

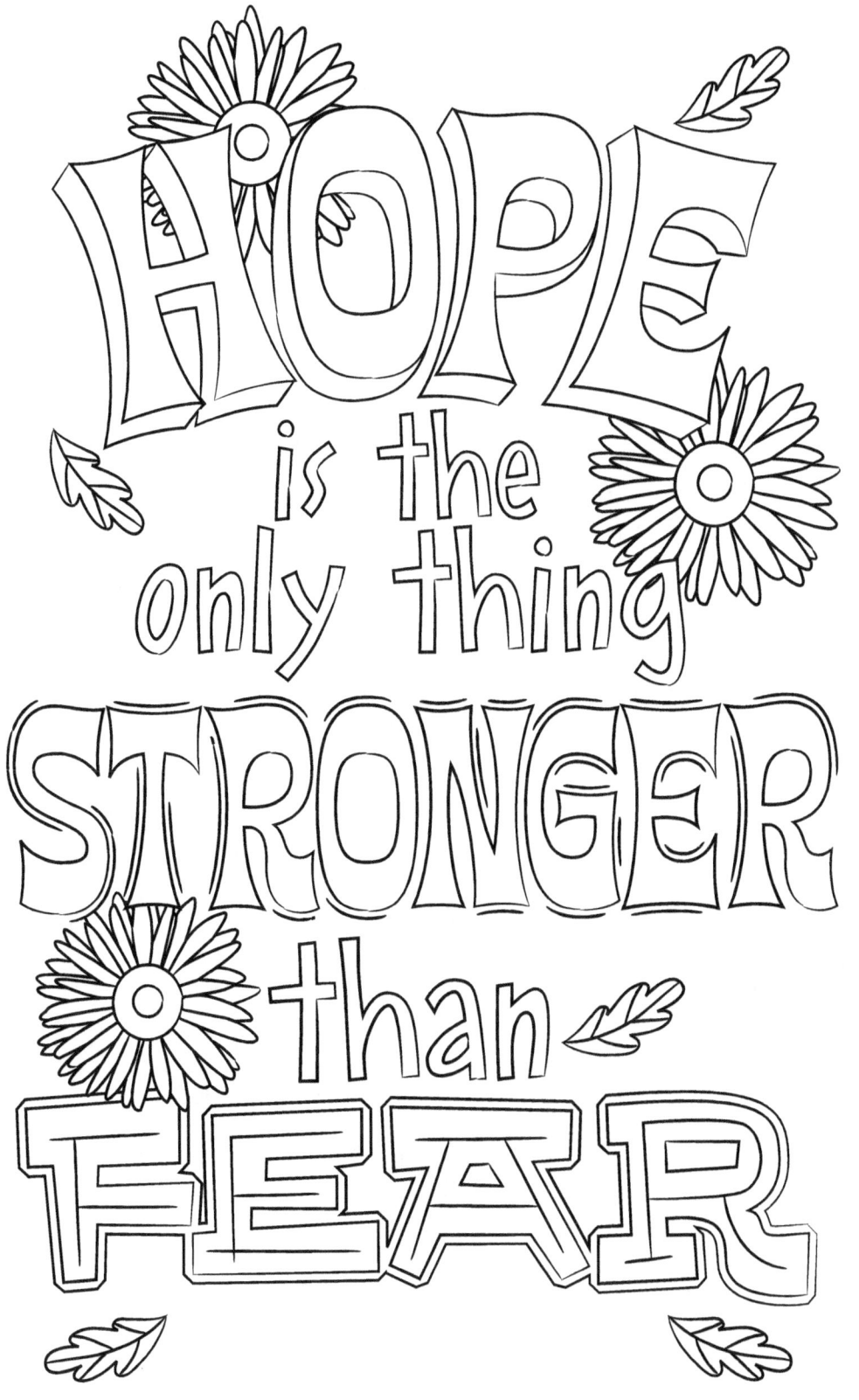

DATE: /   /

DATE: / /

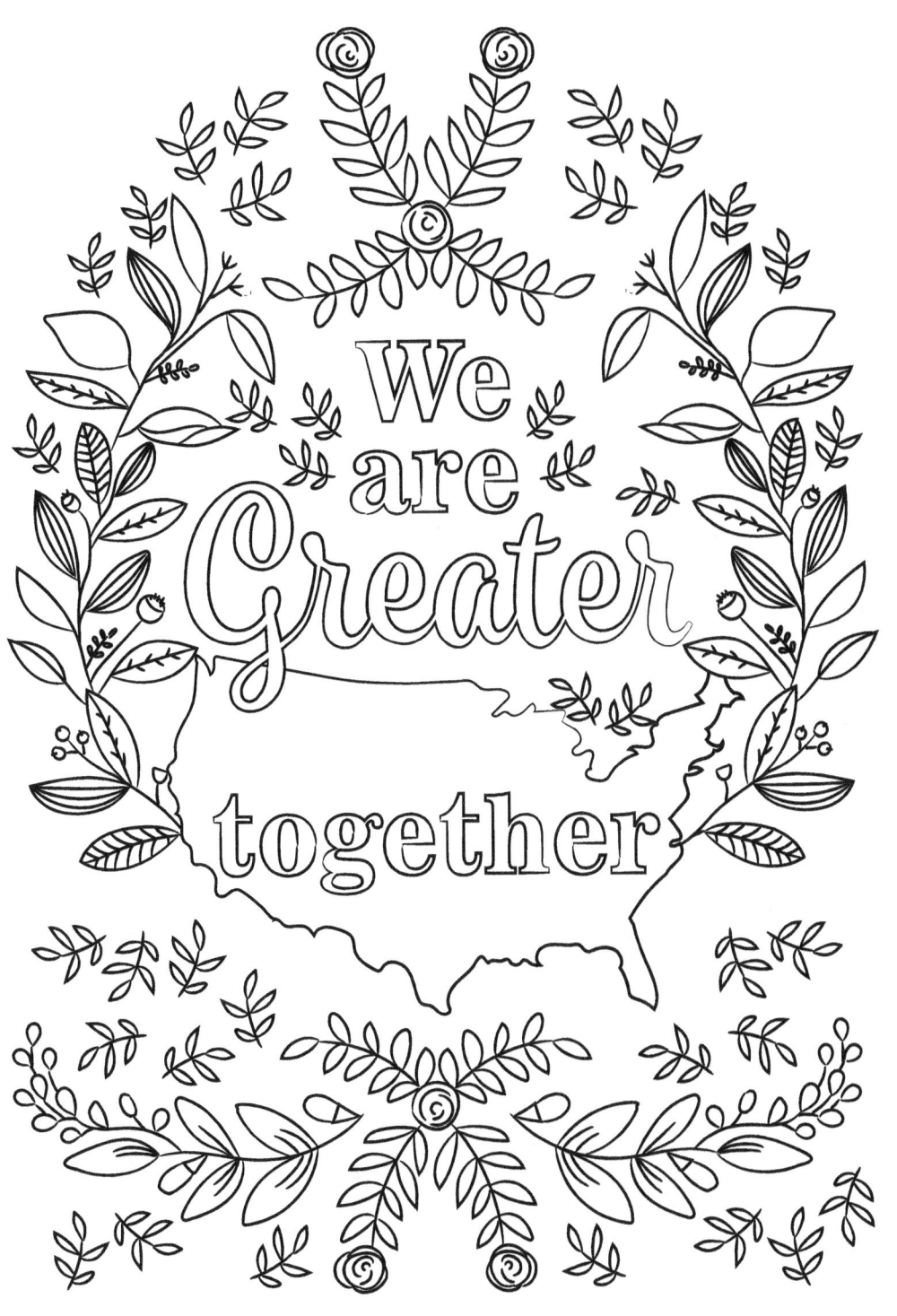

DATE: / /

DATE: / /

DATE: / /

DATE: / /

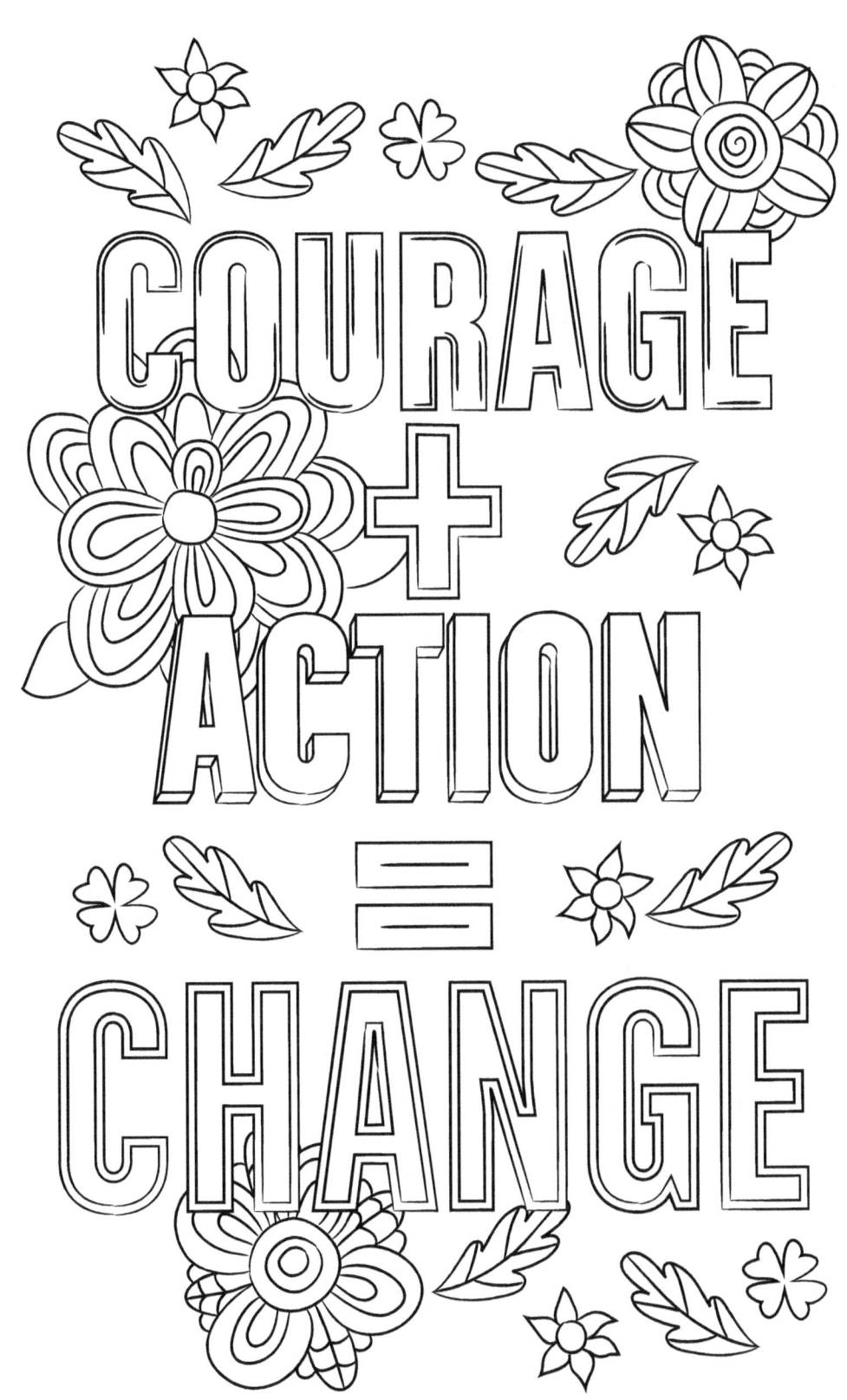

DATE: / /

DATE: / /

DATE: / /

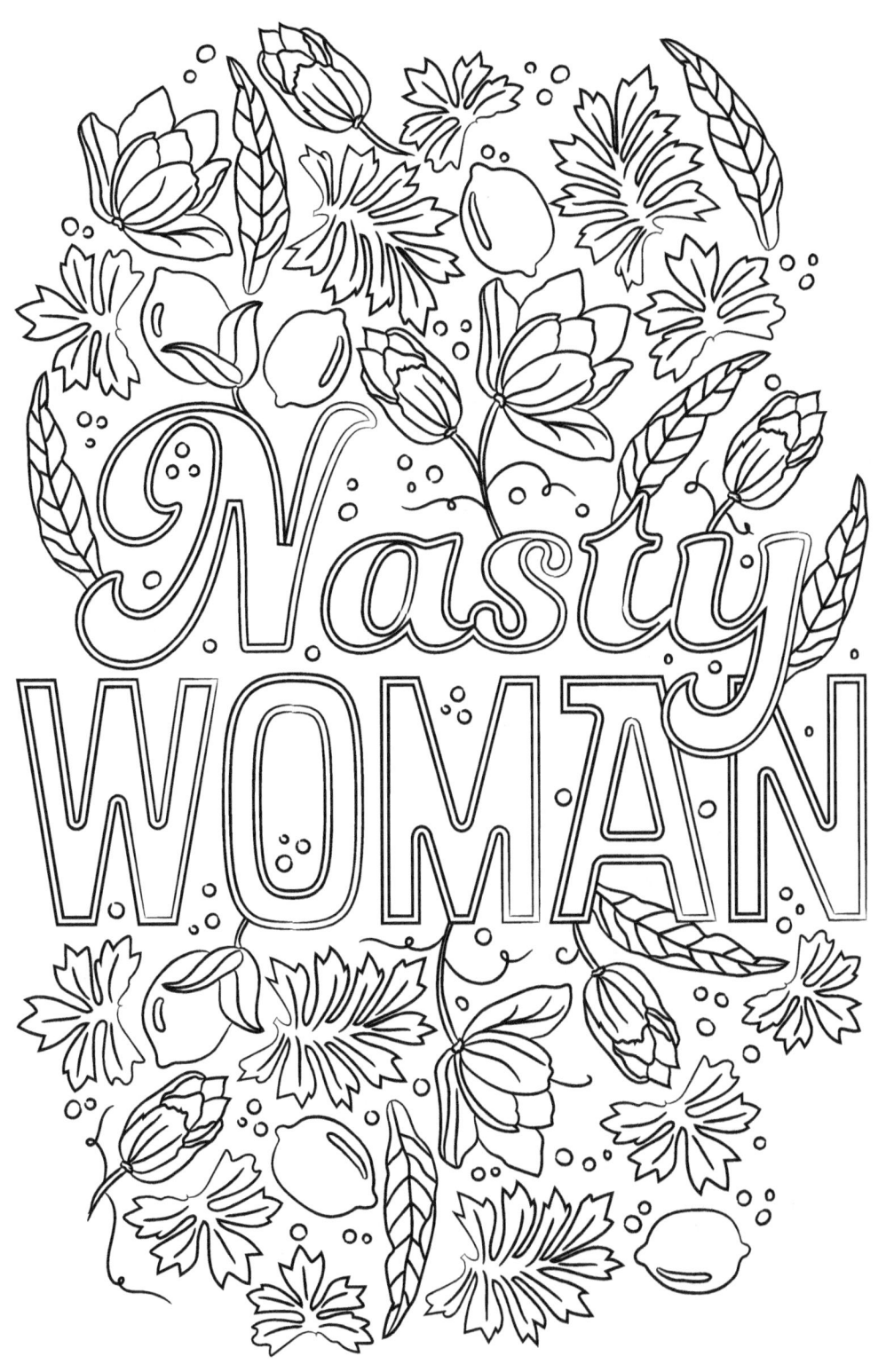

DATE: /   /

DATE: / /

DATE: / /

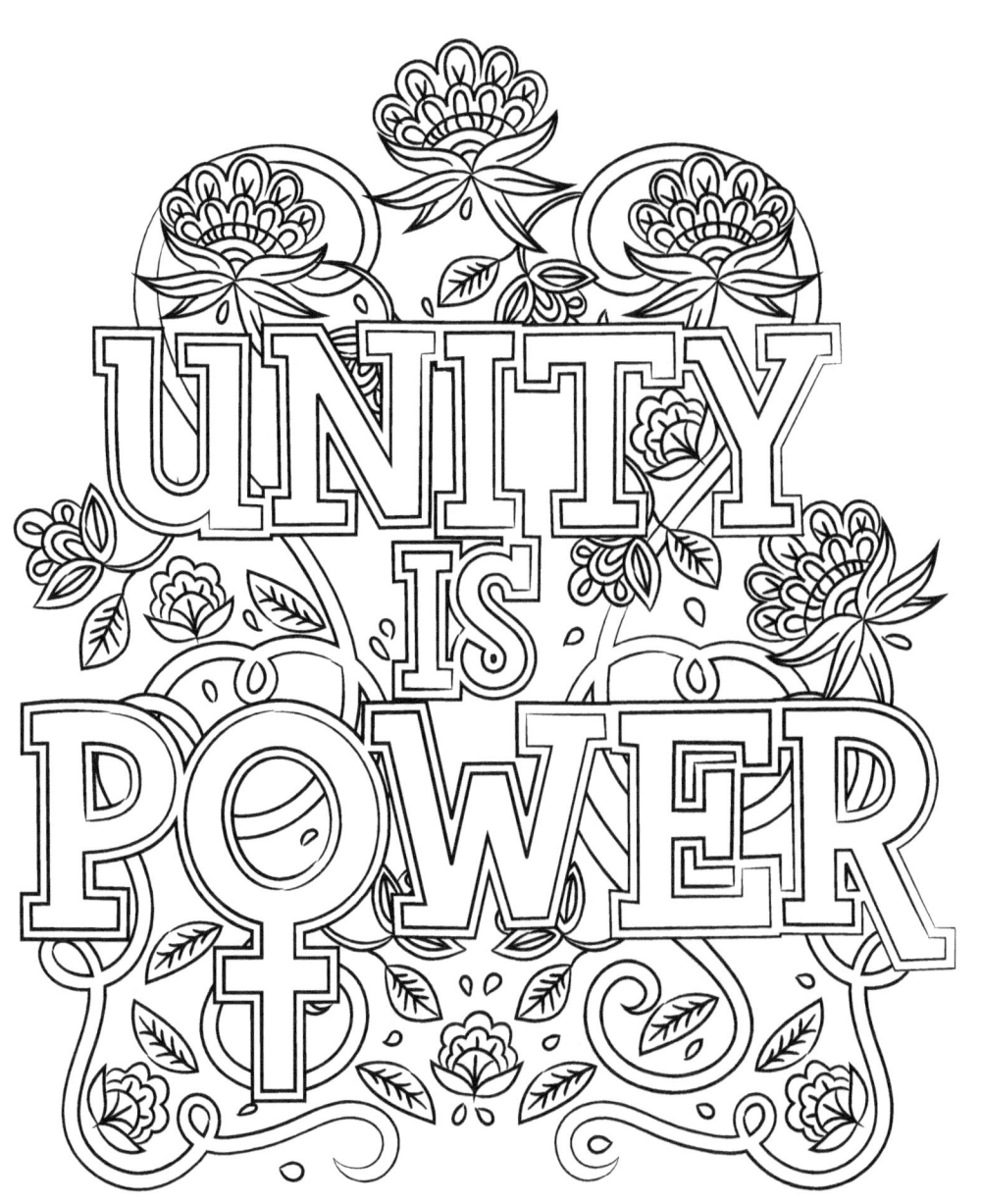

DATE: / /

DATE: / /

DATE: /   /

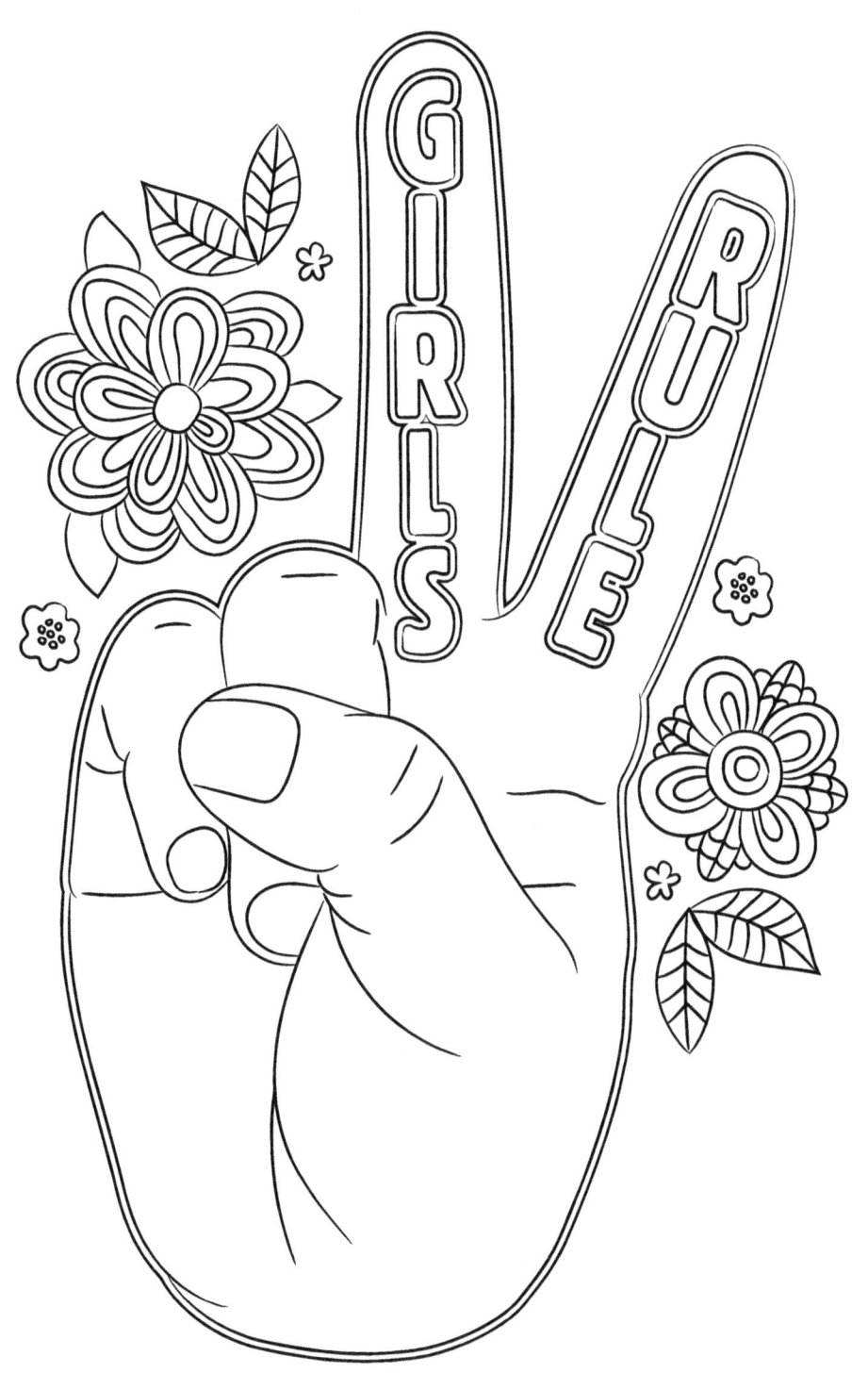

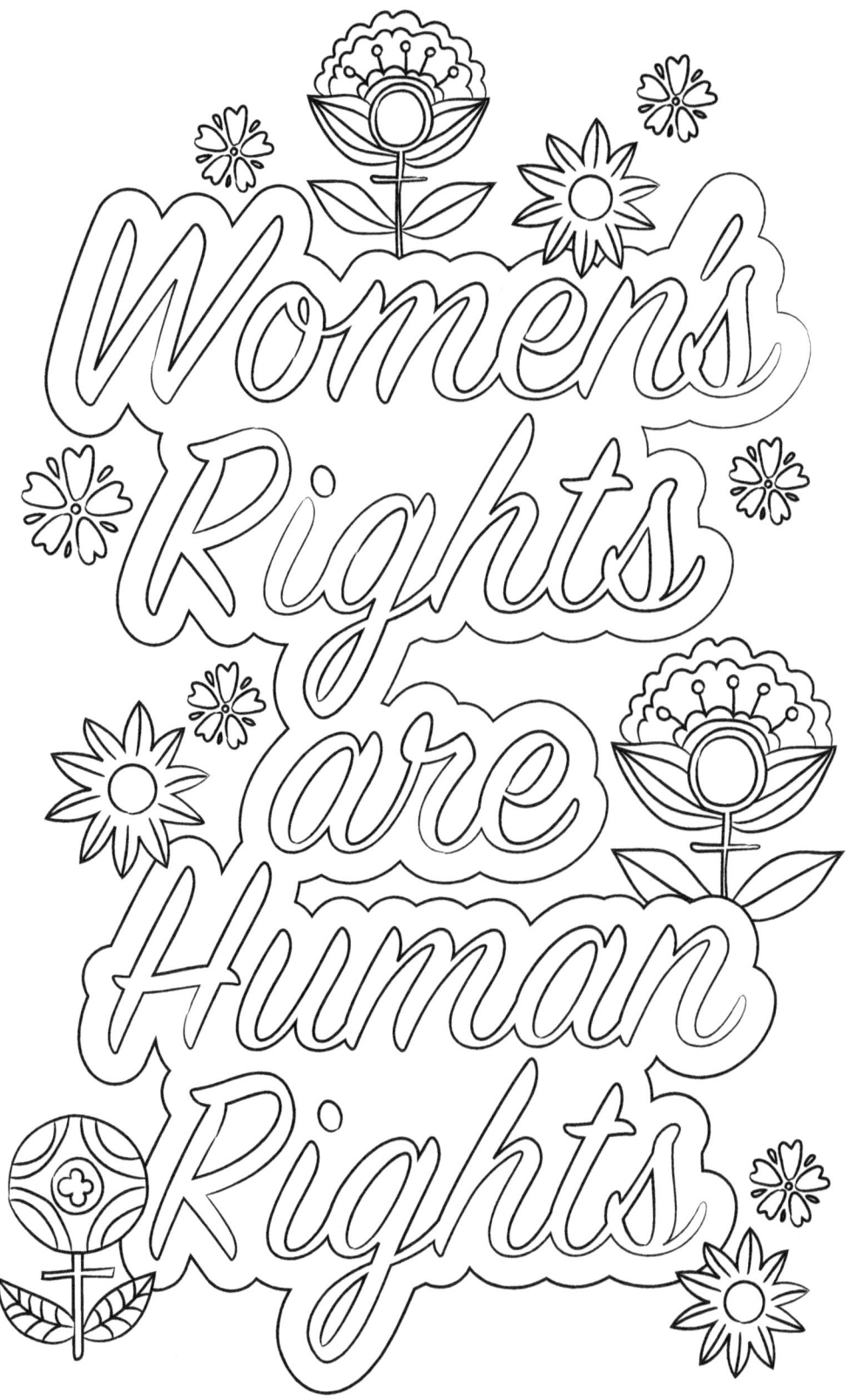

DATE: /   /

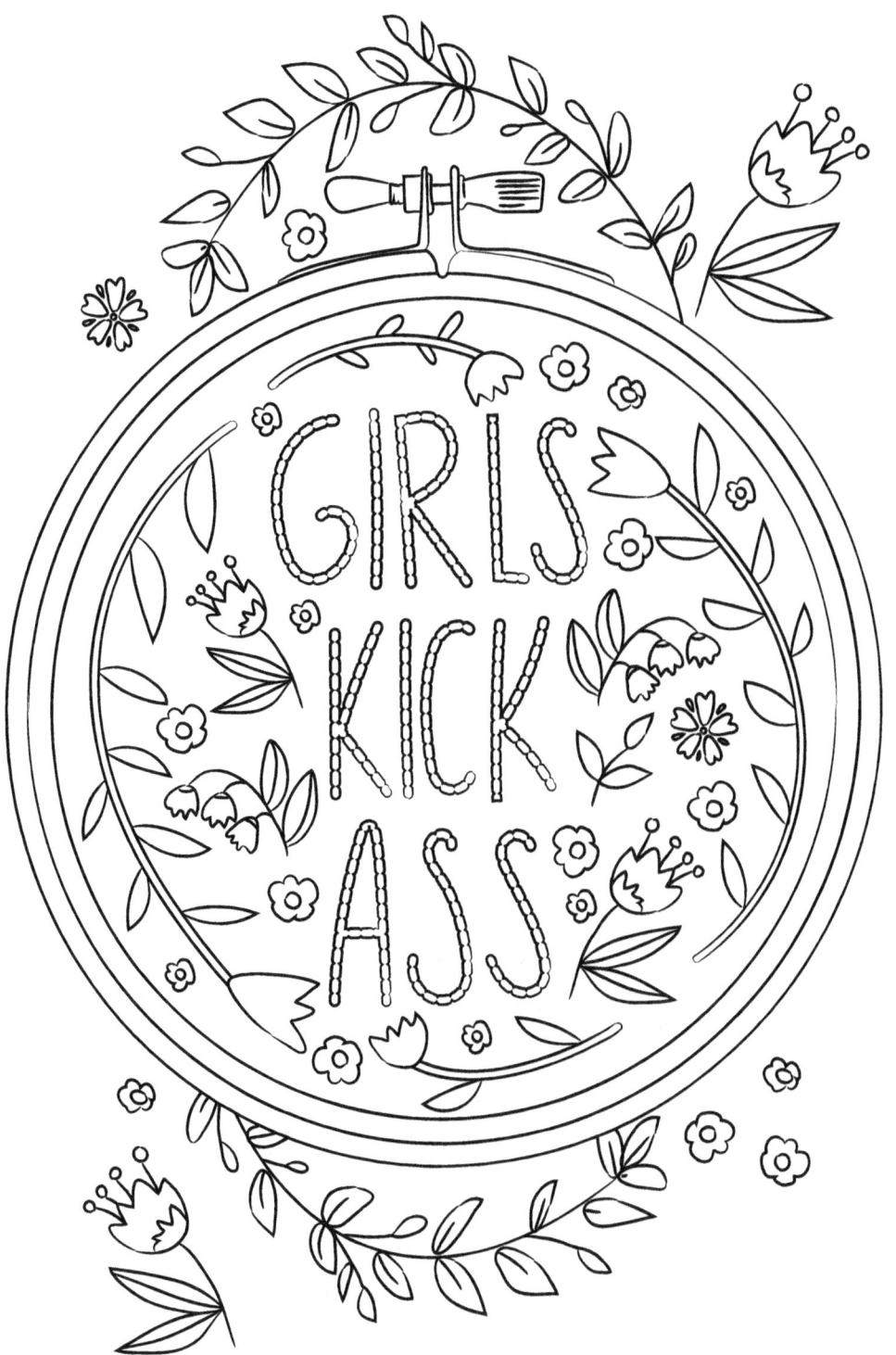

DATE: /   /

DATE: / /

DATE: /   /

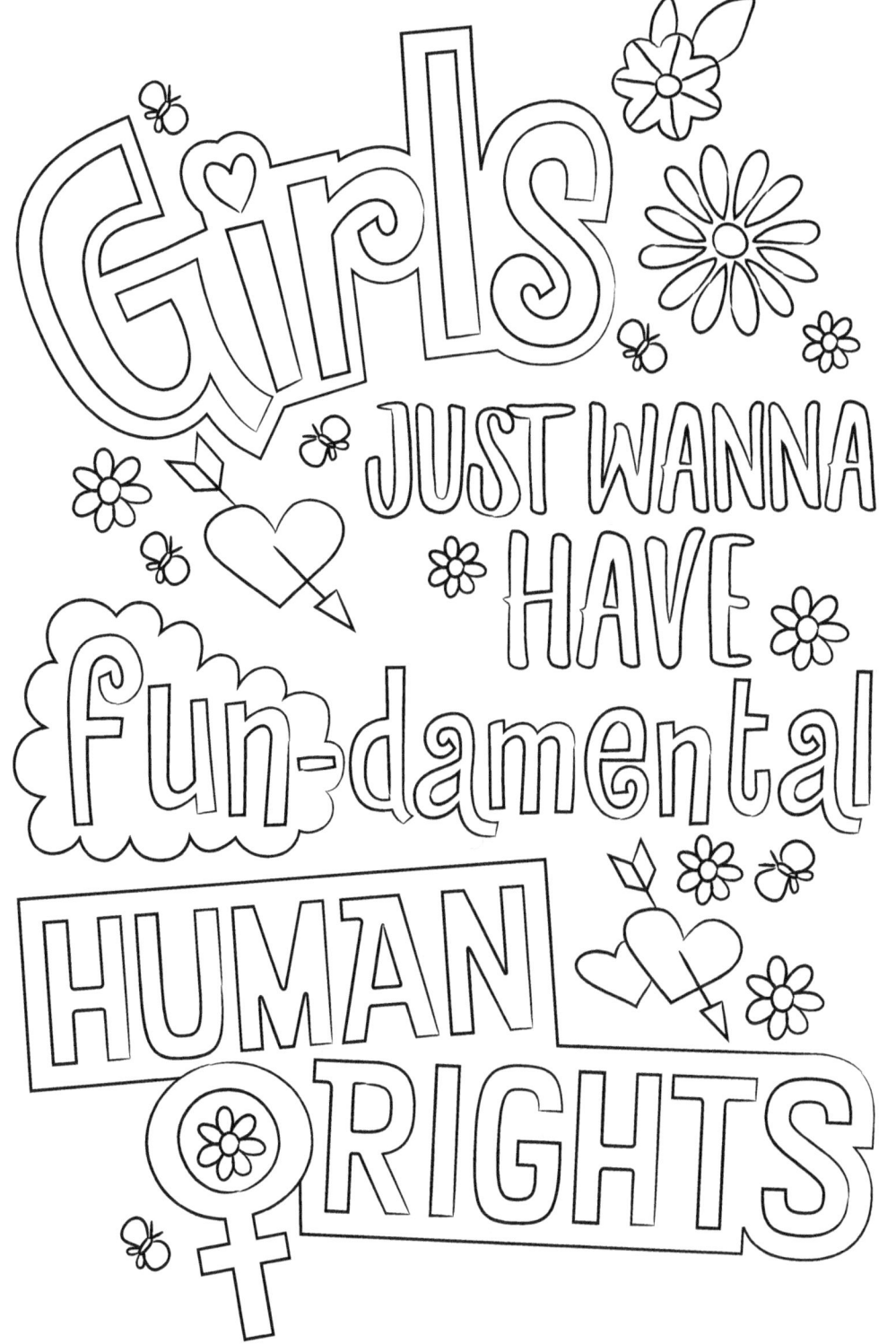

DATE: / /

DATE: / /

DATE: / /

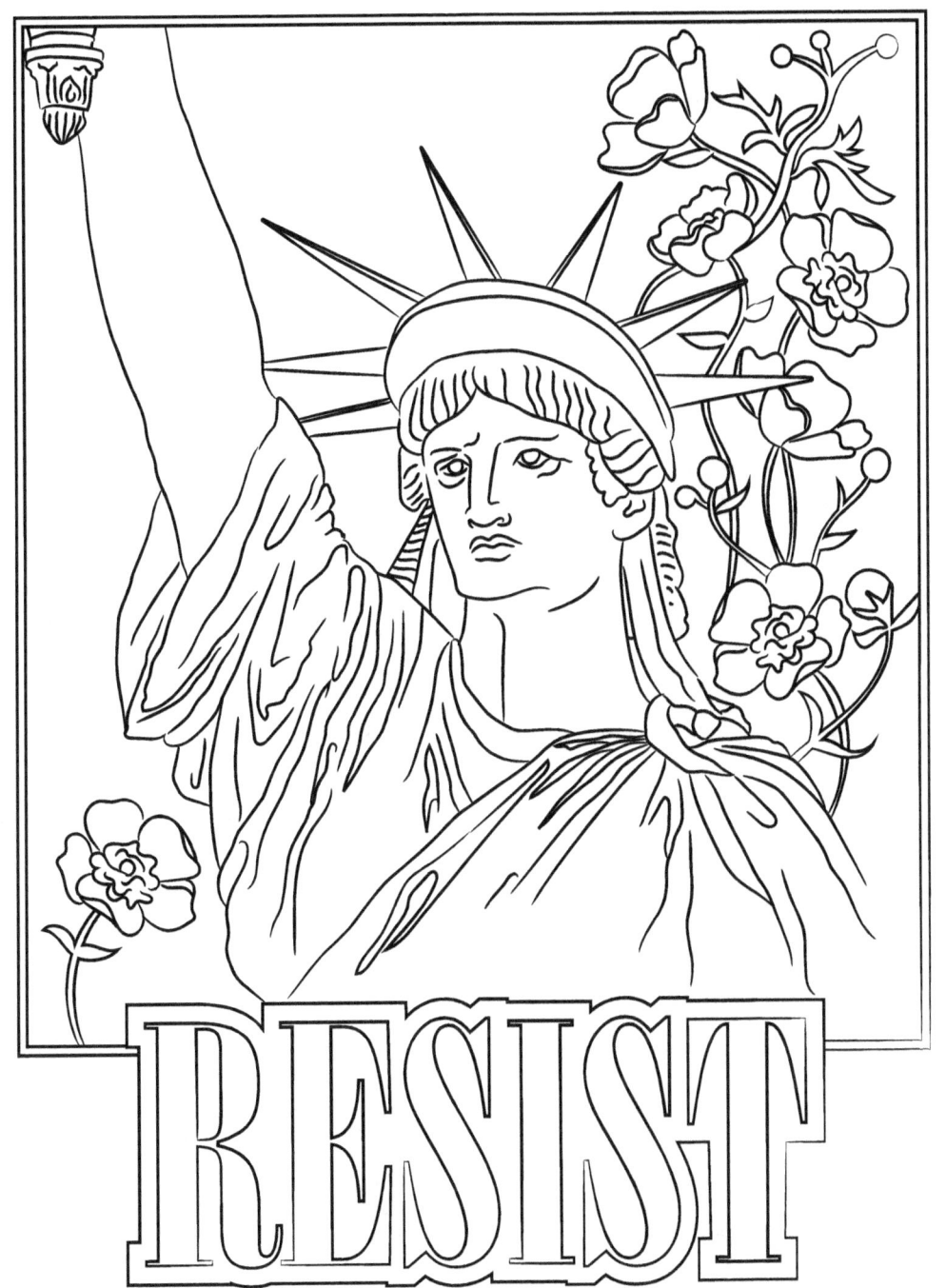

DATE: /   /

DATE: / /

DATE: / /

DATE: / /

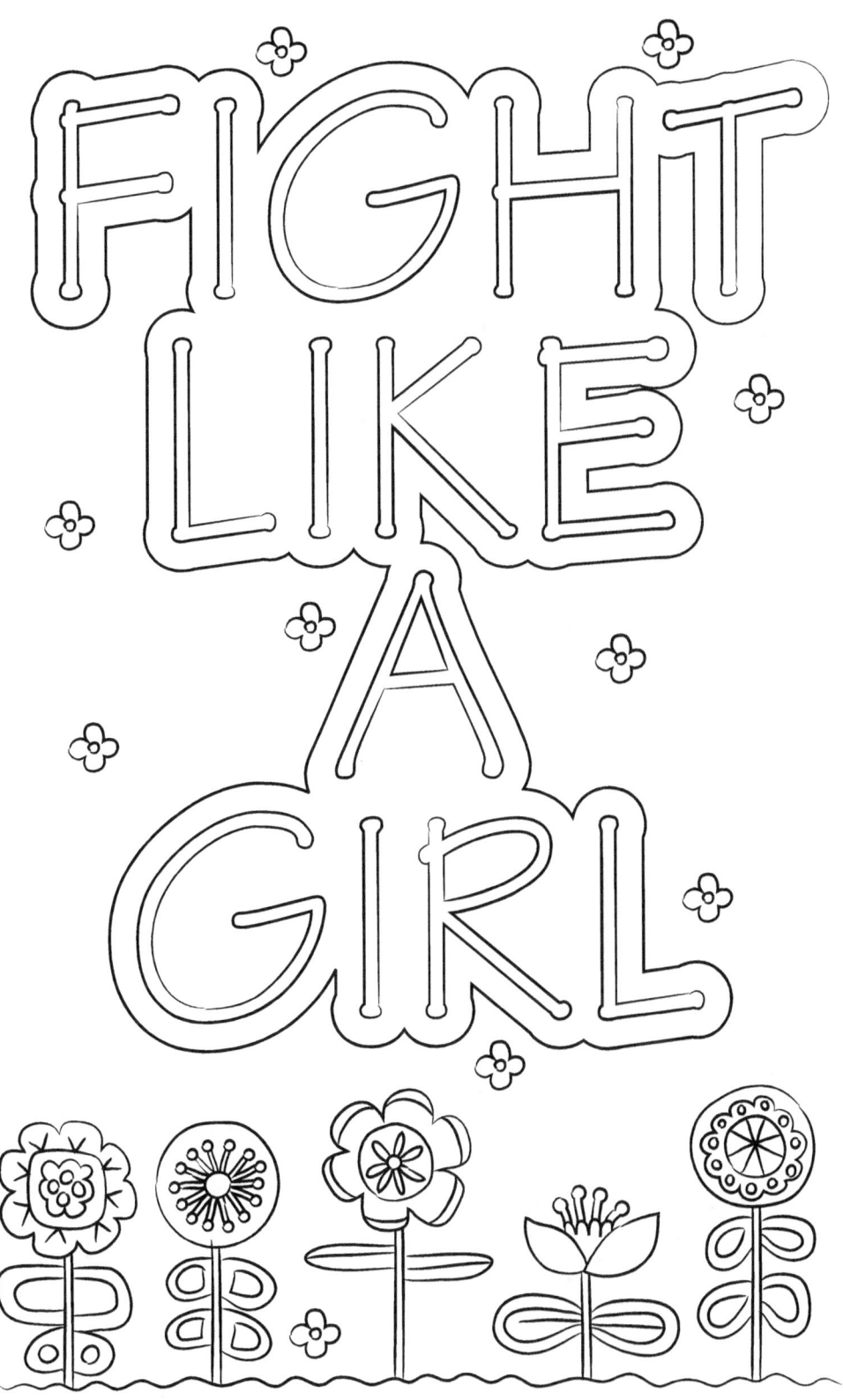

DATE: / /

DATE: / /

DATE: / /

IN ORDER
FOR YOU TO

INSULT ME

I WOULD

FIRST

HAVE TO

VALUE

YOUR OPINION.

DATE: /   /

DATE: /   /

DATE: / /

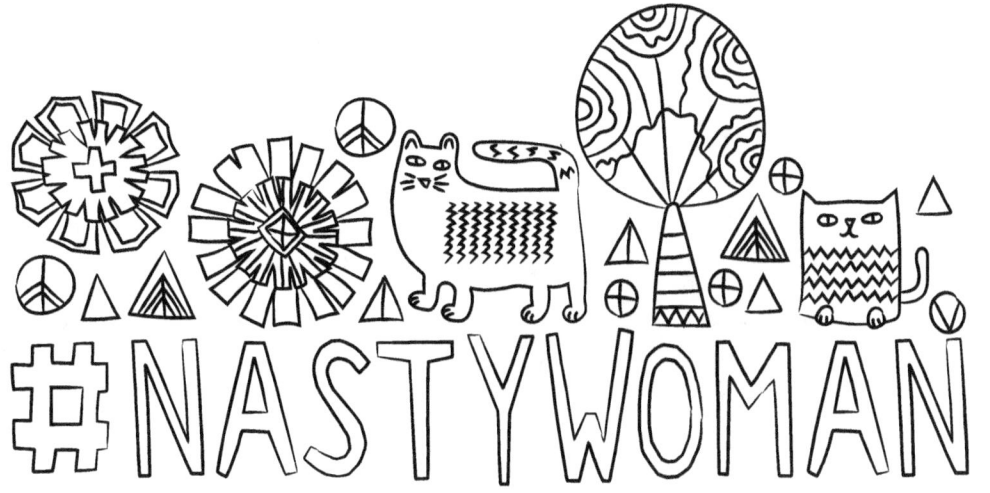

DATE: / /

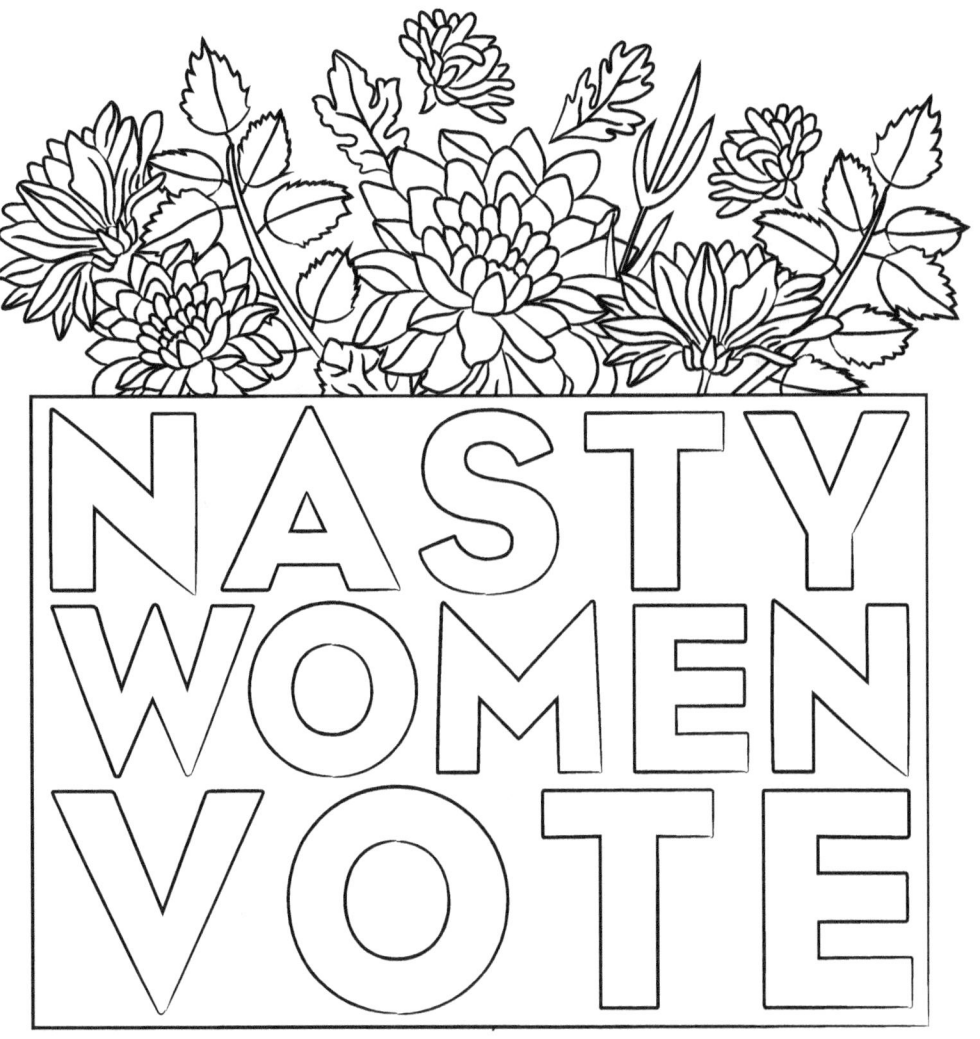

DATE: / /

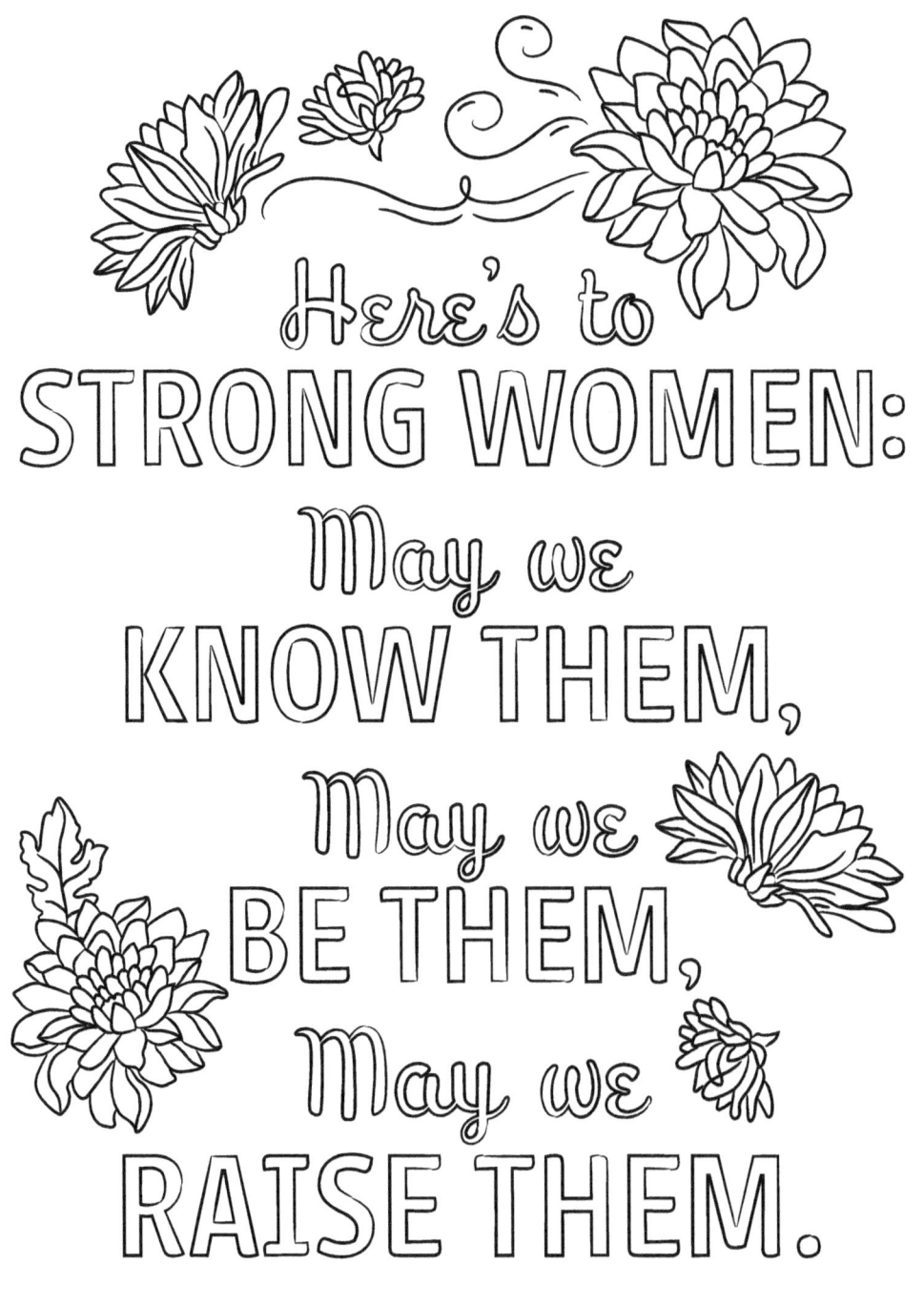

Here's to
STRONG WOMEN:
May we
KNOW THEM,
May we
BE THEM,
May we
RAISE THEM.

DATE: / /

DATE: /   /

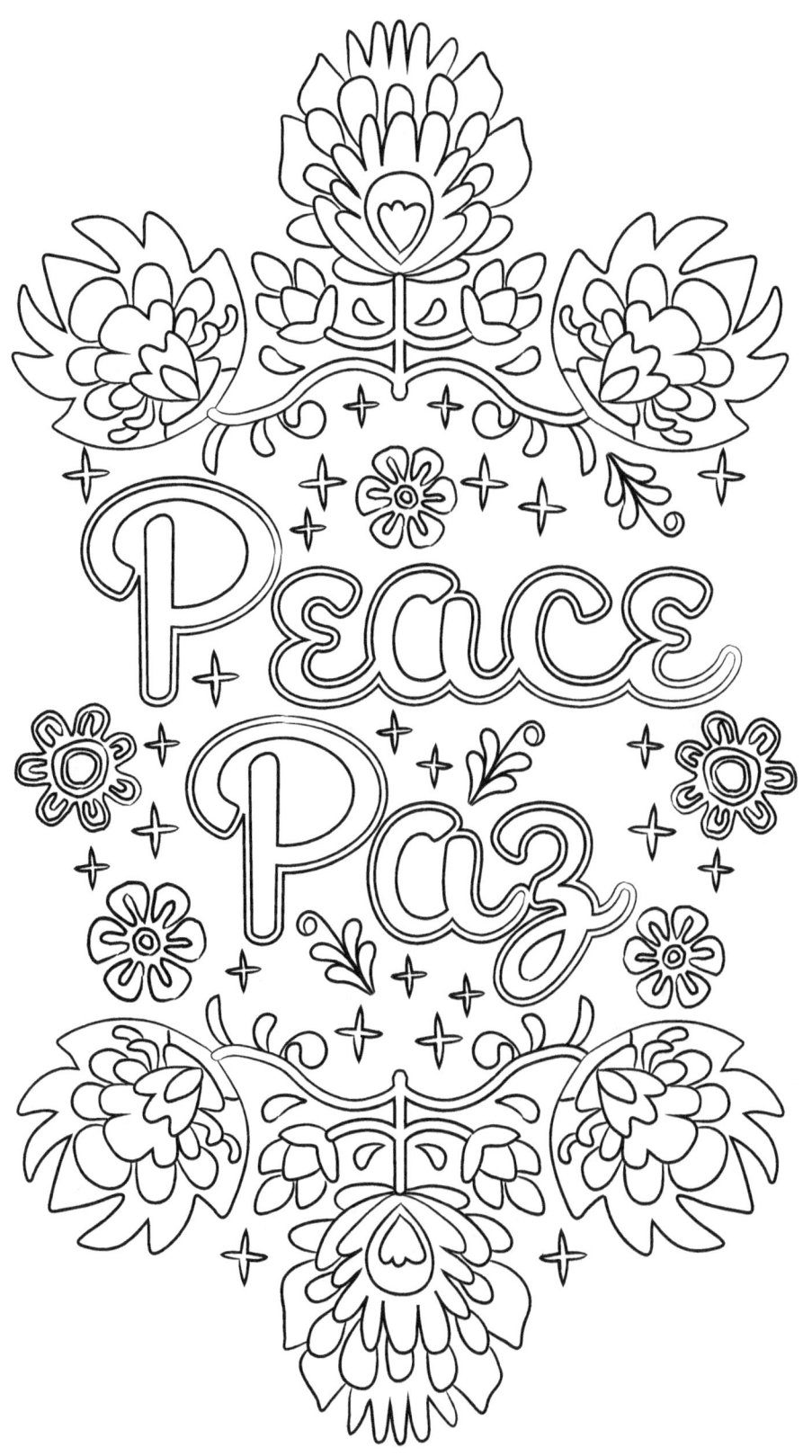

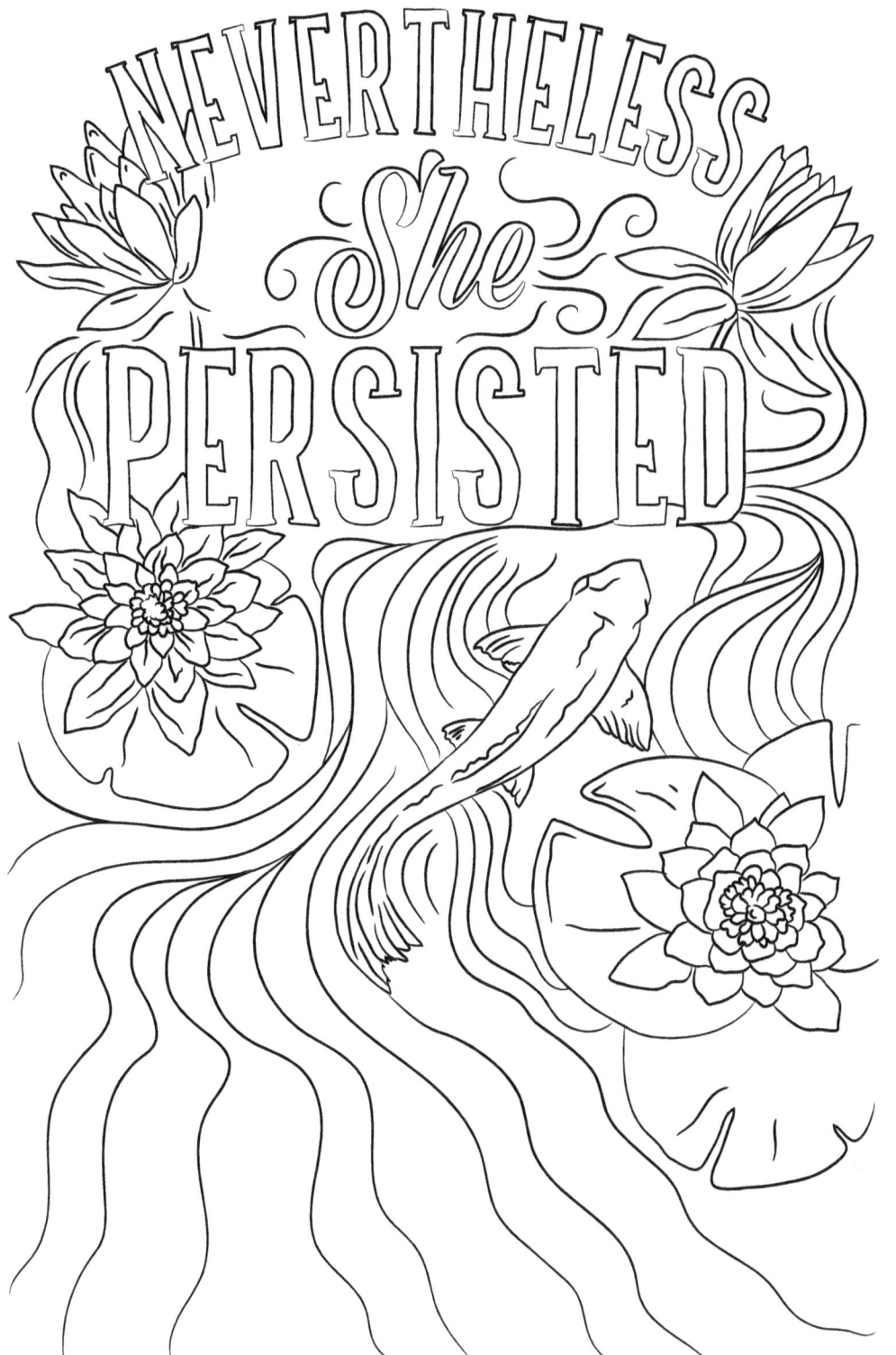

DATE: / /

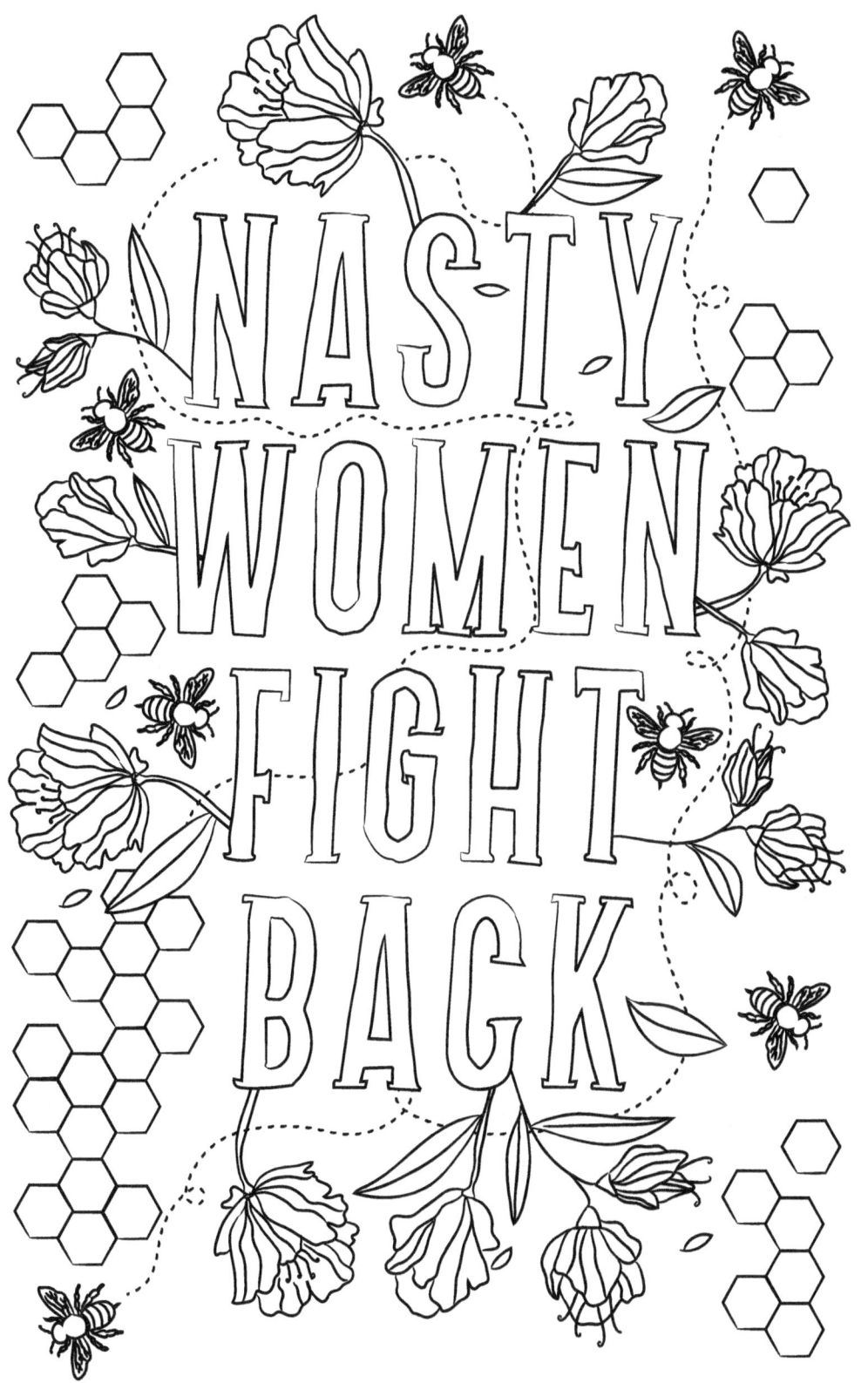

DATE: /   /

DATE: / /

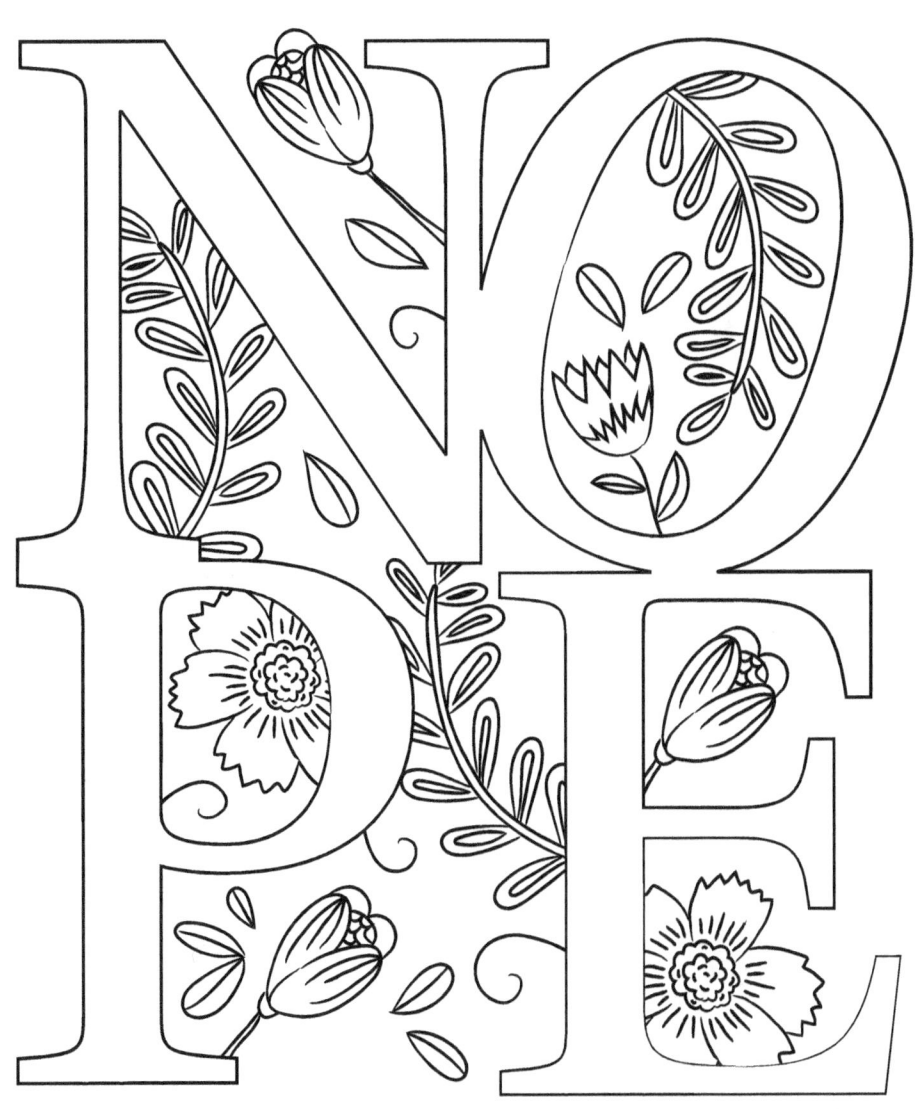

DATE: / /

DATE: / /

It is better
to light
a candle
than
curse
the
darkness.

Eleanor Roosevelt

DATE: /   /

www.ingramcontent.com/pod-product-compliance
Lightning Source LLC
Chambersburg PA
CBHW051315220526
45468CB00004B/1348

* 9 7 8 1 7 2 4 4 0 3 3 7 7 *